Language in Society

Hi Reader,

My name is Nandi. I am a linguist. Linguists like to learn about how people communicate.

I love that people communicate in different ways. This is called *variation*.

Some people think variation is bad or wrong. Linguists, like me, know variation happens because everyone is unique! We think variation is exciting, interesting, and important!

You might communicate like the people in this book. You might not communicate like the people in this book. That is okay!

The way you communicate is awesome.

~ Dr. Nandi Sims

By Dr. Nandi Sims

T0020423

Rourke™

BEFORE AND DURING READING ACTIVITIES

Before Reading: *Building Background Knowledge and Vocabulary*

Building background knowledge can help children process new information and build upon what they already know. Before reading a book, it is important to tap into what children already know about the topic. This will help them develop their vocabulary and increase their reading comprehension.

Questions and Activities to Build Background Knowledge:

1. Look at the front cover of the book and read the title. What do you think this book will be about?
2. What do you already know about this topic?
3. Take a book walk and skim the pages. Look at the table of contents, photographs, captions, and bold words. Did these text features give you any information or predictions about what you will read in this book?

Vocabulary: *Vocabulary Is Key to Reading Comprehension*

Use the following directions to prompt a conversation about each word:
- Read the vocabulary words.
- What comes to mind when you see each word?
- What do you think each word means?

Vocabulary Words:
- *Africa*
- *community*
- *culture*
- *slavery*

During Reading: *Reading for Meaning and Understanding*

To achieve deep comprehension of a book, children are encouraged to use close reading strategies. During reading, it is important to have children stop and make connections. These connections result in deeper analysis and understanding of a book.

Close Reading a Text

During reading, have children stop and talk about the following:
- Any confusing parts
- Any unknown words
- Text to text, text to self, text to world connections
- The main idea in each chapter or heading

Encourage children to use context clues to determine the meaning of any unknown words. These strategies will help children learn to analyze the text more thoroughly as they read.

When you are finished reading this book, turn to the last page for an *After-Reading* activity.

Table of Contents

My Diverse Classroom

Everyone in my class unique.

Everyone in my class talk unique.

Everyone in my class talk different.

Ángel don't speak no English. Ms. Jones don't understand Ángel.

Liu use English and Chinese together. Ms. Jones don't understand Liu.

I speak English, but Ms. Jones don't always understand me.

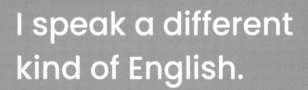

I speak a different kind of English.

African American English

NORTH AMERICA

ATLANTIC OCEAN

enslaved

My English came from **slavery**.

SOUTH AMERICA

EUROPE

AFRICA

Africans

Black folks was taken from **Africa** to the Americas. They was sold as slaves.

They knew African languages.
They had to learn English.

Many Black folks learned a different kind of English. This English called African American English.

In this English, sometimes sounds are different.

Sometimes sentences are different.

de, day, dat

the, they, that

She go to the store.

She goes to the store.

Sometimes whole words be special.

baby hair

I got words for parts of my hair.

Language Is Culture

Most people in my **community** speak this way.

The way we speak is part of our **culture**. It keep us connected to our people.

Some folk don't like when people talk different.

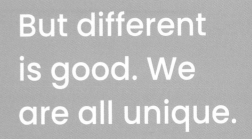

But different is good. We are all unique.

The way we talk is part of who we are.

We all talk different,
and different is good!

Photo Glossary

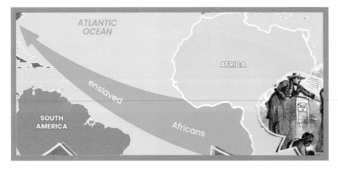

Africa (AF–ri–kuh): a continent south of Europe; second largest continent

community (kah–MYOO–nih–tee): a group of people who live near each other or have shared interests

culture (KUHL–cher): the ideas, languages, and habits of a group of people

slavery (SLAY–ver–ee): the owning of other people

Activity: Language Attitudes

Linguists do research by asking people how they feel about language.

Directions

These two paragraphs tell the same story, but by two different people.

1. Find two or three people to read these stories out loud.

2. Ask them to compare and contrast the writers of the stories.

What do their answers tell you about language attitudes?

Me and my mom, we got a dog. His name Tails. He little. He black. We finna take him to the groomer. His hair been growing too much. He don't wanna go. He all up under the couch.	My mother and I have a dog. His name is Tails. He is little. He is black. We are going to take him to the groomer. His hair has been growing too much. He doesn't want to go. He is under the couch.

Index

About the Author

Nandi Sims earned her PhD in Linguistics from The Ohio State University. She loves to research language variation in communities. When she is not researching, teaching, or writing, she is often dancing or walking one of her five dogs.

After-Reading Activity

Do your words sound unique? Do you have friends who use different words than you? Think of someone you know who might sound different or use different words. Talk with them and listen for the different sounds or words you hear.

Library of Congress PCN Data

Language in Society / Dr. Nandi Sims
(Words in My World)
ISBN 978-1-73165-277-5 (hard cover)(alk. paper)
ISBN 978-1-73165-247-8 (soft cover)
ISBN 978-1-73165-307-9 (e-book)
ISBN 978-1-73165-337-6 (e-pub)
Library of Congress Control Number: 2021952179

Rourke Educational Media
Printed in the United States of America
01-2412211937

© 2023 Rourke Educational Media

www.rourkebooks.com

Edited by: Catherine Malaski
Cover design by: Tammy Ortner
Interior design by: Tammy Ortner
Photo Credits: Cover, p 1 © Monkey Business Images, © Rawpixel.com, © Hill Street Studios, © Dr. Nandi Sims, p 4-5 © Monkey Business Images, p 6-9, © Monkey Business Images, © Vereshchagin Dmitry, p 9 © stockfour, p 10-11, p 22 © Pyty, p 11, p 22 © duncan1890, p 12 © THEPALMER, p 22 © Campwillowlake, © Andrew_Howe, p 13, p 22 © Circa Images/Glasshouse Images Newscom, p 14 © Mangostar, p 15 © Samuel Borges Photography, p 16, p 22 © wavebreakmedia, p 17, p 22 © aldomurillo, © AsiaVision, p 18 © ericcrama, © Jakkrit Orrasri, © Ajdin Kamber, p 19 © iordani, © Monkey Business Images, © michaeljung, p 20-21 © Monkey Business Images, p 24 © Dr. Nandi Sims